Also by Cheri Huber

There Is Nothing Wrong With You: Going Beyond Self-Hate*
The Fear Book: Facing Fear Once and for All*
Nothing Happens Next: Responses to Questions about
Meditation   (former title: The Perils and Pitfalls of Practice)
-*Published by Keep It Simple Books*

✳✳✳

The Key and the Name of the Key Is Willingness*
That Which You Are Seeking Is Causing You to Seek*
How You Do Anything Is How You Do Everything: A Workbook
Time-Out for Parents: A Compassionate Approach to Parenting
(with Melinda Guyol)*
-*Published by A Center for the Practice of Zen Buddhist
Meditation*

✳✳✳

Being Present in the Darkness (former title: The Depression
Book) -*Published by Perigee (Putnam-Berkley)*

✳✳✳

Trying to Be Human: Zen Talks from Cheri Huber*
Turning Toward Happiness: Conversations with A Zen Teacher
and Her Students
Good Life: A Zen Precepts Retreat with Cheri Huber
-*Published by Present Perfect Books (Sara Jenkins, editor)*

✳✳✳

Audiotape
Getting Started, Going Deeper: Introduction to Meditation*

Videotapes by Christa Rypins**
Yoga for Meditators
Yoga for A Better Back
-*Produced by Openings*

*Available on audiotape from Keep It Simple, P.O. Box 91,
Mountain View, CA 94042.
**Also available from Keep It Simple

BE THE PERSON YOU WANT TO FIND

RELATIONSHIP AND SELF-DISCOVERY

Zen Center
P.O. Box 91
Mountain View, CA 94042

Monastery Retreat Center
P.O. Box 1994
Murphys, CA 95247

Published by
Keep It Simple Books
ISBN 0-9636255-2-7

Cover design by Mary Denkinger
Cover art by Sharon Williams

Acknowledgments

Many thanks to all those who keep showing up, looking deeply, and asking questions.

Thanks also to those who read the prepress manuscript and offered insights and suggestions as to how we could make this a better book.

A special thank you to Debra for giving us the idea to write a book on relationships in the first place.

Several of the books I have written are of the pick-up-and-start-reading-anywhere variety. They are loosely organized and conversational in tone.

Much of this book was compiled from talks given at the Zen Center and so has some of those same qualities. For a change, I attempted a beginning-middle-end format and succeeded somewhat. However, you will probably encounter some unexpected twists and turns.

Kind of like life.

And relationships.

Gasshō,
Cheri

ooks on relationship typically ask and answer questions such as the following:

1. How can we understand each other better?

2. How can we be more sensitive to each other's wants and needs?

3. How do we maintain our wholeness and individuality (or develop them) while in a committed relationship?

4. What do we do when one of us wants one thing and the other wants just the opposite?

5. How do I find the "right" person?

6. When we find ourselves in a rut, how do we rediscover the magic?

In this book, we aren't going to give you tools, techniques, and formulas for trying to avoid or fix difficult situations in relationship.

Our interests are awareness and self-knowledge, freedom and mastery. And so we aren't going to answer those questions as such.

Our purpose is
**to help you see through
and be free of
your conditioned responses
to life,**
not find better ways
to operate within them.

To that end, we have restated the questions to reflect how we would approach them. Instead of:

1. How can we understand each other better?

we ask

1. How can I understand myself better so that I can take responsibility for my "stuff" and be more open to my partner?

Consider these restatements:

2. How can we be more sensitive to each other's wants and needs?
2. How can I know what I want and need? Can I give that to myself instead of demanding it from my partner?

3. How do we maintain our individuality while in a commited relationship?

3. What is "individuality"? When are we <u>not</u> maintaining it?

4. What do we do when one of us wants one thing and the other wants just the opposite?

4. Which part of me feels threatened when my partner wants something different from what I want? How can I take care of that part of me without requiring anyone to change?

5. How do I find the "right" person?
5. Can I be the person I want to find?

6. When we find ourselves in a rut, how do we rediscover the magic?
6. What is "magic"? Where does it reside? How do I keep myself from it? Does it come and go, or do I?

Do you see? ⇨

4

Relationship can mirror
   who we are
      if we are willing
         to see it that way.

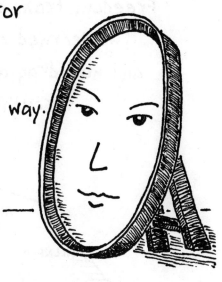

All things can.

And the practice of seeing everything as a
mirror of who we are

opens the door
to freedom.

Freedom from what? ⇨

Freedom from all the "stuff"
we learned as children
and now drag along with us
through life.

Virtually none of it
was true back when we learned it,

and it hasn't improved with age.

Relating to others can be really hard, and it is also often hard to relate to ourselves.*

But why is this so?

From our perspective it's because
   -we have been taught to believe
      many things that aren't true,
   -we don't know how our
      conditioning effects us daily,
      hourly, moment-by-moment,
   -we don't know who we really are
   -we are afraid to find out who we
      really are

   so we focus on and examine the other person's "stuff" and the relating breaks down.

* which is truly the first and most important step

7

If we see clearly
how our ability to remain
open, honest, and loving
with ourselves breaks down,
we have

BIG CLUES

about how that happens
when we try to relate to others.

And so ultimately this book is about
taking 100% responsibility
for our experience
100% of the time.

It is about using everything in our lives--
everything--to see who and how we are, to
accept that, and let it go.

Why would we want to do that?

Because then we are free to live in **this**
moment, open-hearted, and less
encumbered by the past.

                              And because
when we can see how what we were
taught to believe limits us,
we discover a universe of possibilities
we only dreamed existed.

In the Beginning...

I fall in love and find
    that I have tapped
        into the very best within me.

I am loving, generous, and understanding.
Life is easy, bright, and joyful.

I don't mind:

        traffic,
        paying bills,
        my co-workers,
        household chores...

I'M IN LOVE!

BIRDS ARE SINGING!

THE SKY IS BLUE!

THE SUN IS SHINING!

THE FLOWERS ARE BLOOMING!

CHILDREN ARE LAUGHING!

EVERYTHING IS PERFECT!

A little time passes and the stress of the heightened energy of being in love begins to take its toll.
What was spontaneous and thrilling begins to feel a little chaotic.

All the things I've let slide are starting to feel overwhelming.
I miss my structure,
my own habits and schedule,
my friends and family,
my workout,
having the Sunday paper to myself.

Instead of being carefree and joyous, I am irritable, edgy, and bristly. Before this relationship, life was calmer and more predictable. I wasn't required to be available and generous all the time. I had time off to rest and recuperate, time for me, for my life, for who I am.

Now I find I have tapped into the very worst within me. And I'm not aware of exactly what has "gone wrong." I can't find a balance, I lose my ability to communicate, and I go into my survival behaviors.

I become bitter,
        angry,
                resentful,
                        and punishing.

Instead of trying desperately to figure out how to fix the "problem,"
here is the great potential:

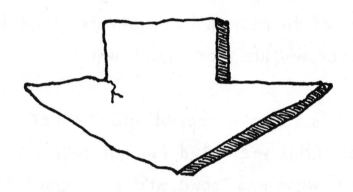

If I will see relationship as a way of discovering more fully who and how I am, I have a chance to return to the kind, loving best in myself through
conscious awareness
rather than through
unconscious conditioning.

1) What is the best part of being in love?

2) What is the worst part of being in love?

3) What do you let slide?

4) How do you stop taking care of yourself?

5) What are some of your survival mechanisms?

The Five Processes

To help see more clearly how we are in relationship, throughout this book we will use the five tools, or processes, listed below. These processes are the foundation of awareness, which is the secret to a successful relationship.

1. belief systems and assumptions
2. projection
3. identities (aspects of the personality)
4. disidentification
5. centering

Each is explained in the following section.

Belief Systems
and Assumptions

(These are sometimes hard to recognize.)

As children we were taught to believe many things about life, love, ourselves, and just about everything else.

We are almost completely unaware of these beliefs that are the basis of our sense of who we are,
our decisions,
our relationships with others,
our assumptions about why we are even on the planet.

It rarely occurs to us to question our beliefs and assumptions.

They color all our thoughts and perceptions and yet we are remarkably ignorant of them.

Examples of beliefs:

Relationships require compromise.

I will grow up, meet the right person, fall in love, and live happily ever after.

If I am nice to people, they will be nice to me in return.

If I work hard and do a good job, I will be appreciated and rewarded.

When I do something wrong, I should punish myself.

Add your own:

Where do our beliefs come from?

Are they useful?

Are they true?

As we look out at the world, we constantly tell ourselves a story about what we are seeing.

The U.S. should maintain a strong national defense.

The look she just gave me means she's interested.

That carpet looks terrible with that sofa.

The New Age means humankind is moving in the right direction.

Art today is just junk.

We need to return to the values of our ancestors.

Homeless people aren't trying.

We should not be destroying the environment.

The story I make up about the world is based on my beliefs and assumptions and nothing else.

If I am unaware of this, I think my story is pretty much true, that I am perceiving things as they are, or as they should be, and as everyone else perceives them.

From all these
  completely conditioned,
    never examined,
      contradictory,
        questionable
          baffling,
            points of view,

I _project_ my beliefs, ideas, and opinions
onto everyone and everything and further
believe I truly know something.

Projection
(not from a camera, from our heads)

verything is a mirror of ourselves. We always see ourselves when we look out at the world and other people. It is not possible to experience and label anything that is not a part of ourselves. Is this always true? Always.

When we are unaware of this process, we believe we are correct in our assessments. We believe there is an objective reality "out there" from which we are separate and about which we can know something.

In projection,
this is what we tend to do:

We project the worst and best of
ourselves.

1)   I project the worst of myself onto
people I dislike, don't respect, and can't get
along with.   --"She is narrow, closed,
humorless, and irritating."

2)   I project the best of myself onto
people I admire, love, and want to be
around.   --"He is open, generous, kind, and
compassionate."

What I do not accept in myself,
I do not accept in another.

                    What I accept in myself,
                        I accept in others.

In the first circumstance,
it is good to become clear about what it is
in the other person that is so
unacceptable and difficult for me →↓

←←←←←←←←←←←←←←←←

↳and follow that back to myself.

This is the reason most of us will elect to
get rid of the other person before it
comes to that.

In the second circumstance,
it is good to become clear about what it is
in the other person I like and admire but
feel I don't possess →↓

←←←←←←←←←

↳and follow that back to myself.

This might also be a reason we get rid of
the other person before it comes to that!

Think of someone you like and admire.
What are three of their qualities?

1)

2)

3)

Think of someone you don't like or admire.
What are three of their qualities?

1)

2)

3)

Can you see how you are each of these
ways?

P.S. If you can't see them right now,
please begin to look for them. If you are
feeling really courageous, ask someone who
loves you to help you see these qualities
in yourself.

It is sometimes possible to see our projections in this form:

If I believe certain behaviors mean someone is being selfish, and I see someone exhibiting those behaviors, without question I will label that person "selfish."

When I am "identified with a part of me" who feels she knows selfish actions when she sees them (and probably tries to avoid acting that way herself), I am operating out of an <u>identity</u>.

Identities
(We all have bunches of them.)

e use the word "identity" to refer to a part of the personality. Others might use the terms "role," "persona," or "subpersonality" to point to the same thing.

Identities most often manifest as voices in our heads. For example, many people, after beginning an awareness practice, notice they have an internal judge who constantly tells them what they and others

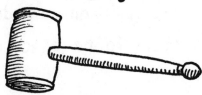

have done wrong. Many report an image monitor who makes sure they don't do and say embarrassing things. The "inner child" is an identity, and almost all who look closely find many inner children. Other identities many share include the worker,

the sports fan, the family member, the
perfectionist, the worrier, the free spirit.
The list is almost endless.

Interestingly enough, we have
many aspects of our personalities who
completely contradict
each other. A part of me might be
frugal, and another part, extravagant.
Another might thrive on taking risks, while
its opposite wants safety and predictability.

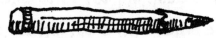

Can you find pairs of identites in yourself
who seem to be exact opposites?

Describe them.

Identities are defense systems, survival
mechanisms. They tend to appear when
they are needed. Phrases such as
   "Leave your work at the office,"
   "Don't send a boy to do a man's job,"
   "I'm just not myself today,"
   "Part of me wants to do that and part
    of me doesn't,"
reflect our understanding that we play
many roles and assume various identities.

If we want our spiritual path to lead to
freedom and mastery, having a detailed
understanding of who and how we are, and
how we got to be that way, is very
helpful. Using this "identities" model helps
us see our conditioning in small, discrete
segments instead of as a whirling mass of
conflicting data...

Will I stay or will I go? I want people. I feel so privileged. I am so annoyed. I should quit my job. I wish my life were easier. I must please I need more money.

If nothing else, using this model as a means of exploring the self shows us there is no one "self" that can be pinned down and relied upon under all circumstances. There are many, many parts--aspects of the self-- and they all have the same name: I.

A number of people at the Zen Center have for years been looking at themselves using this "aspects of the self" or "identities" model as a means of making sense of the seeming contradictions so many of us experience inside ourselves. We requested them, if they chose, to draw verbal portraits of the parts of themselves who are most present in intimate relationship. Some described pairs of identities; some described one; most gave them names.

The format was simple: state the identity's main belief, what s/he projects, the self-talk that goes with that, the benefit and liability of having this part, how the identity is recognized, and what happens when you are no longer identified as this part.

Here are some of the identities they described for us:

"The Romantic"

> **MAIN BELIEF:**
> Love is all. The object of
> my affection is the reason to live.

PROJECTION:
The Adored is perfect and brings all
wonderful things to life.

SELF-TALK:
"If I have this person, I'll have everything.
Then I'll be happy."

BENEFITS:
Great passion, romance, fantasy

LIABILITIES:
She lives in a dream world; she is often
disappointed.

HOW SHE IS RECOGNIZED:
She is obsessively attentive.

WHAT HAPPENS NEXT
The disappointment grows and I become
"What About Me?"

"What About Me?"

> **MAIN BELIEF:**
> Everyone else gets all the good stuff.
> When do I get a turn?

PROJECTION:
Nobody cares about ME.
SELF-TALK:
"I'm sick of this. I'm going to start taking
care of me, not someone else."
BENEFITS:
She keeps me from losing myself, from
giving myself away completely.
LIABILITIES:
She "keeps score" and becomes bitter,
angry, and self-righteous.
HOW SHE IS RECOGNIZED:
The feelings of resentment.
WHAT HAPPENS NEXT:
I remember not to be resentful. I get
enthusiastic about something else.

"Steady & Stable"

> **MAIN BELIEF:**
> Jump in with both feet or don't jump at all.

PROJECTION:
Those who don't give their all in relationship are insincere.
SELF-TALK:
"I will do whatever it takes to make this last for the rest of our lives."
BENEFITS:
She is willing to go through the hard things that come up in relationship.
LIABILITIES:
She confuses merging with commitment.
HOW SHE IS RECOGNIZED:
I envy couples in long-term relationships.
WHAT HAPPENS NEXT:
The envy gets to be too much and I become "Flesh & Flash."

"Flesh & Flash"

> **MAIN BELIEF:**
> Monogamy and fidelity are not natural human traits.

PROJECTION:

Long relationships lose their passion.

There's no romance in them.

SELF-TALK:

"I feel trapped. Life is too short to say no to these feelings."

BENEFITS:

Life rarely stagnates.

My wardrobe looks better.

LIABILITIES:

Life can seem shallow, meaningless.

HOW SHE IS RECOGNIZED:

Other people become sex objects.

Weight loss

WHAT HAPPENS NEXT:

Physical and emotional exhaustion

"Married Mitch"

MAIN BELIEF:
Life is better if you share it with
a companion, a soul-mate.

PROJECTION:

People who don't have someone are
unfortunate. They are missing life.

SELF-TALK:

"This is great.
I'm the luckiest guy in the world."

BENEFITS:

Life has a steady quality to it.

LIABILITIES:

There is always someone else around
whose feelings have to be considered.

HOW HE IS RECOGNIZED:

His focus on home and hearth.

WHAT HAPPENS NEXT:

I start wanting time alone, and "Single
Sammy" takes over.

"Single Sammy"

MAIN BELIEF:
Commitment means
I will have to compromise.

PROJECTION:
"Happiness is being single."
SELF-TALK:
"It's my life, my time, and my money and
I want to spend them on me."
BENEFITS:
Autonomy, independence, self-reliance
LIABILITIES:
I become egocentric, idiosyncratic, and
stuck in my ways.
HOW HE IS RECOGNIZED:
He is social and friendly but lacks any
special connection with people.
WHAT HAPPENS NEXT:
Life begins to feel too cold.
Loneliness begins to sneak into his days.

"The Child"

> ## MAIN BELIEF:
> If I am good enough, my partner won't get mad at me.

PROJECTION:
She is angry and unhappy and it is my fault. Her feelings depend on me.

SELF-TALK:
"She's unhappy. How can I fix this?"

BENEFITS:
He is tender and has the ability to be playful and light.

LIABILITIES:
His efforts to fix everything cloud our ability to see where we are.

HOW HE IS RECOGNIZED:
Tight chest, short breath.

WHAT HAPPENS NEXT:
I feel my body tighten when my partner becomes angry and unhappy.

Now it's your turn.

"(Your Identity's Name)"

MAIN BELIEF:

PROJECTION:

SELF-TALK:

BENEFITS:

LIABILITIES:

HOW S/HE IS RECOGNIZED:

WHAT HAPPENS NEXT:

If you would like, duplicate this page for each relationship identity or pair of identities you recognize in yourself.

It is not at all uncommon to become "stuck" in an aspect of the self and to be unaware of being stuck. When we are completely identified with one part of the personality, there is little, if any, awareness other viewpoints exist. "This is how I am, I've always been this way, and I'll always be this way," is a common feeling. This is projected outward onto the world, which can make for a very static, deadened, some would say safe, existence.

The next MAJOR STEP in spiritual practice is to learn to **disidentify**.

Disidentification
(long word, simple concept)

Disidentification is the action of "stepping back" from an identity and viewing ourselves from a greater perspective. It is actually a common experience. Almost all of us have suddenly realized that we are watching ourselves from "above" or from someplace "outside" ourselves. We didn't choose this, it just happened. It is possible, with practice, to learn to disidentify at will.

Why do that, you ask? Read on.

Charlie: Before becoming aware of the process of disidentification, I always assumed my thoughts and feelings were the real me, who I really am.
So any time I had a thought-emotion combination (ex: This is unfair; I feel angry),

UNFAIRNESS
↓
ANGER
↓
EXPLOSION

I had no choice but to respond in the way I had been conditioned to respond.

It was simple: When I thought this or felt that, my response was automatic, and that's what I would do.
   It never occurred to me not to!

As I have begun to disidentify at will, I can simply be present as
   thought-emotion-conditioned response combinations arise. I can be a witness to that movement within me,
not a victim to it.

When learning to disidentify, we often step back into just another aspect of the conditioned self and find that we are stuck in suffering, spinning our wheels as usual.

Again,
with practice,
we can learn to recognize when this happens, disidentify again, and return to center instead.

Charlie: If I am angry, for instance, and I step back from the feelings, thoughts, and energy of that anger and find I am judging myself for being that way, alarms go off in my head: "Judge alert! This guy is just another identity! Disidentify again! Return to <u>center</u>!"

Centering
(common word, not so common experience)

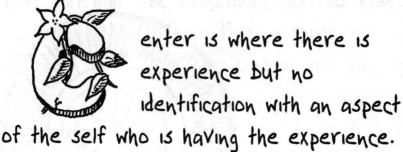

enter is where there is experience but no identification with an aspect of the self who is having the experience.

What?

Being at center is being in this moment.
Open. Present. Aware. Awake.
Not controlling. Not resisting. Not believing.
Holding onto nothing. Pushing nothing away.
No "better ideas" about how it should be.
No illusion of separation.
No illusion of an "I"
who exists outside the moment.

What we are pointing at here is that
THIS IS IT!

And remember:

Awareness is

never

judgmental.

If you are judging or being judged,
another of your identities is at work.

As the five processes:

> projection
> beliefs and assumptions
> identities
> disidentification
> centering

are mentioned throughout the book, they will often be in **bold** letters. We hope you will refer back to these pages to more fully comprehend their meaning.

Survival

A definition of intelligence is the ability of an organism to adapt to its surroundings. Children are intelligent. They adapt swiftly, accurately, and completely when they need to.

As we grow up, we constantly absorb ideas and opinions, **beliefs and assumptions.** These define us; they become our identities.

Finish these sentences.

I believe ____
I am a person who ____
I like ____
I disapprove of ____
People should ____
To be okay, I must have ____
I cannot ____

The more of these ideas I maintain
about who and how I am, the more

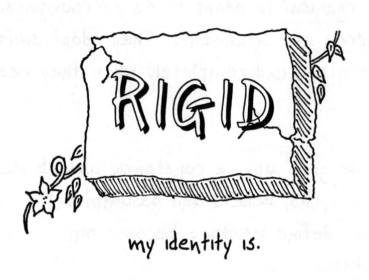

my identity is.

I **project** constantly from these identities,
these parts of myself, and the positions
they hold.

How I see the world at any given point
depends on which part of me
I'm identified as.

I see people, places, and things

in particular ways

based on the attitudes of the identities

that developed when I was a child

as I adapted to my surroundings

in my attempts to survive.

(Whew!)

The sad, strange,
unfortunate, dysfunctional part is that,
as adults,

most of us are still trying
to survive childhood.

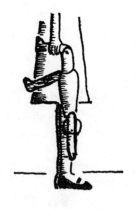

So,
I have become the person I believed as a child I needed to become in order to make it through to adulthood.

Now,
I'm an adult, I'm in an intimate relationship, and I'm suffering! This is traumatic! I have picked, consciously or not, someone who is going to relive parts of my childhood with me, who is going to play the parts opposite me someone else did back then. I'm going to suffer in the same way I did as a child, and

I am going to use
the same survival mechanisms.

Look at the following situation.

 You come home from work and announce that you have two tickets to the theater. We could have a nice dinner somewhere, then go to the play, then go for a walk in the park.

 I went to the video store on my way home from work, picked up a great movie, bought a six-pack of beer, and ordered a large veggie deluxe pizza that is due to be delivered in 15 minutes.

Our worlds collide.

You envisioned a wonderful, exciting, romantic evening on the town. When you discover that I have a pizza-beer-video evening planned for us,

your heart drops to your toes.

You're diasppointed. You're frightened by what this means. "I'm afraid we're too different. I'm afraid you'll never be the person I want. How can I be the person you want? How can I tell you I don't want to do what you've planned? How can I tell you I want you to do what I've planned? I don't want to be controlling. I don't want you to feel bad or guilty, but I really don't want to do what you want to do."

At this point, childhood survival strategies usually kick in. Anger? Tears? Defeat? Rejection? Withdrawal? _____?

From conscious awareness there can be great sympathy for this person. There can be understanding of her enthusiasm and excitement, her romantic dream, everything she hopes for, what she has wanted all her life--and the tremendous disappointment she feels, and the fear, when she doesn't get what she wants.

This doesn't make her a bad person. It makes her a conditioned person.

So there I am, quite proud and pleased with my little plan. I actually went out of my way for this, and I know that you are going to be pleased with me. This is indeed going to be a romantic evening.

Then you come in with these tickets, and I feel like an oaf. "We are just too different. I'm not sure we're right for each other. I finally do something I think is going to really work and it all falls apart before it even gets started. I wonder why I should even try."

Again, this is the point at which survival mechanisms from childhood surface.

From compassionate awareness there can be complete understanding of this person's desire to do good and be good and be loving and do the right thing and make a special effort, and then be really frustrated and let down, feeling kind of foolish and defensive.

This doesn't make him a bad person. It makes him a conditioned person. He is someone who is caught up in old stuff instead of being in the present moment-- but he is not a bad person.

From a place of compassionate awareness for oneself, it is easier to project the same goodness and innocence onto one's partner. It is easier to see that we are both in identities. We can see that we both wanted the same thing--to enjoy each other's company, to feel close and loving, to have a nice life. How we go about that is sometimes very different, but from compassionate awareness, we have the vision and clarity to be in the present, not victimized by childhood conditioning.

In this book,
we aren't going to give you tools, techniques, and formulas for trying to avoid or fix these kinds of situations.

Our purpose is
to help you see through and be free of the survival system,
not find better ways
to operate within it.

When you don't get what you want:

How do you act?

How did you act as a child?

Are you afraid? frustrated? angry? _____?

How do you communicate your feelings?

What happens next?

Why can't people get along?

People can't get along because we have each gone through a process of socialization. We have all been molded to fit into a family structure, but the details are different for every person alive.

We all start out just how we are, and then we are

> changed,
> fixed,
> improved,
> and altered

until we become something different.

"We are all born charming, fresh, and spontaneous, and must be civilized before we are fit to participate in society."
- Miss Manners -

The problem is that these family structures vary greatly. Whether it's an Orthodox Jewish or a Southern Baptist household, whether working class or wealthy, young or old, drunk or sober, educated or uneducated, close or distant,
it doesn't matter.
We are molded.

It happens to all of us.

And we belieeeeve this stuff we are taught. Deeply. In fact, it's so ingrained in us, it doesn't actually require belief.

We never question it.*
This is reality.
There's no doubt about it.

*Even if we rebel against it.

This is an analogy we use to illustrate
what growing up and being taught to
conform is like:

I am in a play.
The play is my life.
I don't know that it is a play,
or that I am being taught virtually all my
lines, actions, and behaviors.

This play is the only reality I know. I have
no awareness of any other possibility. As
far as I can tell, I am who I think I am,
and I'm making my own choices. I have no
memory other than being on this stage, in
this cast, expected to know my lines, and
to fit into the action of the play.

So, why can't people get along?
Keep reading.

We now introduce you to
BOB and ELLEN.

(You will encounter them throughout the book.)

Baby Bob is born in rural Arizona, and he learns to fit into his family structure. He learns to perform his part in the play.

Meanwhile, Baby Ellen is born in suburban Connecticut, and she does the same in her family. She learns her cues and memorizes her lines.

For each, THIS IS REALITY.
This is how life is.
Their own particular play is the world.

Bob and Ellen grow up, meet, and fall in love.

They are intelligent. They know people have their differences, but they are alike in many ways, and so, **without any conscious awareness**, assume they have a strong foundation to build upon.

In the beginning, they find their differences... charming.

Time passes and that little illusion dissipates. Each begins to notice the other sees life a little too differently. Each realizes their assumptions about common ground are far from correct.

Bob
wants to live
in the country.

Ellen has never even entertained the idea
but is willing to give it a try.

Before long, she gets over it.

Ellen
wants to keep
their finances separate.

Bob has never thought much of the idea
but is willing to give it a try.

Before long, he gets over it.

Because we are all,
each and every single solitary one of us,
attached to

being right,

conflict results.

RIGHT

in Bob's play is not the same as
RIGHT

in Ellen's play.

They value opposing things and interpret actions and words opposite from each other. Both are willing to tolerate (at best) the other's dissimilarities

for a while.

But each believes, fundamentally, the other is WRONG.

Before long,
each begins to question,

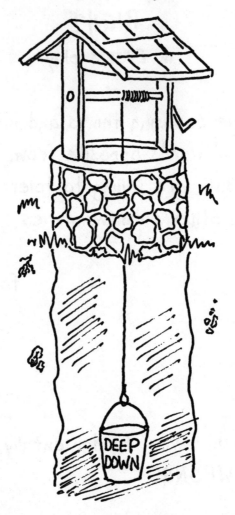

"If this is who you are,
if this is really how you think,
I'm not sure I want to share
my life with you."

"Wrong" is defined as:
    doesn't support my identity
    puts me in touch with who I'm
        trying not to be
    threatens who I think I am
    brings out feelings I try to avoid
    and on and on...

Example:
Bob wants to watch TV and eat pizza, and
Ellen deeply and perhaps unconsciously
believes that is wrong. And, yes, she does
try to be understanding of people's
differences, but this is too close to home.
She believes the right people read books,
are interested in ideas, are concerned
about their diets. At the very least, if
you are going
to eat pizza,
go to a nice
Italian restaurant.
Don't eat in front of the television.

We believe our conditioning so deeply, when we run into something that opposes it, that thing is wrong. (AND when _we_ do not live in keeping with our conditioning, we believe we are wrong.)

As children, learning to fit in, adopting the beliefs and values (or their opposites) of the authority figures around us was literally a matter of survival.

As adults, we are still carrying that around with us. We react to threats to our identity as if our survival were at stake. Therefore, if I have thrown my lot in with yours, and you prove to be too different from me, I must conclude you are wrong. This is the only way I can keep my identity intact, the only way "I" will survive.

This is why people can't get along.

And so the question we must ask is:

Would I rather defend
learned behaviors and reactions,
or would I rather open my heart
and be in the moment?

This is the aspect of relationship that
makes it a spiritual issue.

Example: The person I live with is not as tidy as I am. When it comes down to it, I can hold on to my ideas about "tidy," I can defend my learned position (which just might cost me my relationship), or I can explore my learned reaction. I can look at what goes on with me when things are not the way I want them to be, when external circumstances do not match up with my internal programming.

I can learn how that operates within me, make peace with that, and open to a whole variety of responses other than my narrow,

    confining,

        limited,

            programmed reaction.

In this, I have the possibility of opening my heart to embrace this person whose conditioniing is different from mine. I can open my heart, and together we can look for ways to resolve this tidiness issue.

Or I can close my heart and continue to believe there is some inherent right/wrong issue about tidiness,
defend that,
stay stuck,
be unloving and probably unloved.

We are not saying I have to be less tidy or my partner has to be tidier. No one needs to give up anything.

This is not problem-solving.
This is awareness practice.

And awareness practice, from our point of view, aims at freedom from suffering.

71

When I am no longer concerned with
   who's right and who's wrong
   who's good and who's bad
   who's at fault and who gets credit,
when I am no longer threatened when
someone wants to live in ways different
from me, I can be open enough to find
solutions to the problems. Until then I
am
   so attached to my conditioning,
   so concerned with controlling
     another's behavior,
   so determined to get my way,
   so convinced I am right,
I have little hope of affecting a truly
loving solution.

What is an issue, such as tidiness, that causes discord in your relationship?

What are your **beliefs and assumptions**, your self-talk, your **projections**?

Which of your **identities** holds this as an issue?

How might this issue look from **center**?

Would you be willing to **disidentify**?

Can you feel compassion for the part of you, the identity, who is struggling with this issue?

Okay.

So then, people come to an awareness practice like ours looking for something to make their lives better.

And they have all kinds of ideas about how that will happen, but, essentially, that's what they want.

We try to get them to step outside the framework of their conditioning, to see that

> how they are is the result
> of what happened to them,
> not who they intrinsically are.

To stay with our "life is a play" analogy, we ask people to come down off the stage, sit in the audience, and from there watch the play as it unfolds.

The tricky part is we ask them <u>to watch themselves perform</u>, just as they have been taught, without changing anything. This is **disidentification**, and it gives them a larger perspective.

It begins to dawn

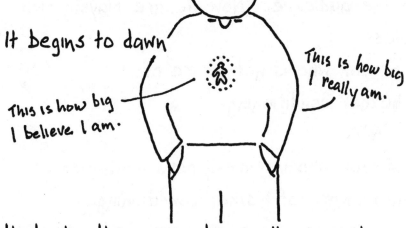

This is how big I believe I am.

This is how big I really am.

that who they are intrinsically is much greater than who they were taught to believe they are.

And, first and last, the thing we must be aware of is <u>judgment</u>.
                              If we are watching ourselves in the play and judging what we see, we never actually made it off the stage.

If we change from actor to drama critic,
we stopped short of making it all the way
to the audience. Now we are playing two
roles:

person-who-is-not-aware-of-
his/her-conditioning
AND
person-who-is-judging-person-who-is-
not-aware-of-his/her-conditioning.

In this analogy, being "in the audience" is
being at **center**.
No judgment.
    No better ideas.
        No plans to fix anything.
Just conscious, compassionate
    awareness and acceptance,
        noticing how this actor is
           in this moment.

The secret
is to become conscious, aware, and present
to how we cause ourselves to suffer.
Then all of life becomes practice. Our
biggest stumbling blocks are the judgments
and beliefs we have about what we see
when we start looking at ourselves with
conscious awareness.

The missing element is compassion.

If we can simply see,
with compassion,
all that arises within us,

we dramatically increase
our chances of moving
away from suffering.

What does that mean? To illustrate, remember the "dinner-theater-walk" versus "video-pizza-beer" collision (p.52)?

WANTS TO GO TO THE THEATER	WANTS TO WATCH A VIDEO
Has envisioned an exciting, high-energy, romantic evening on the town	Has envisioned a cozy, quiet, restful, romantic evening at home
Is pleased with herself for getting the tickets and planning the evening	Is pleased with himself for renting the video and planning the evening
Is sure her partner is going to be pleased with the plan	Is sure his partner is going to be pleased with the plan

THEIR WORLDS COLLIDE

EACH FEELS...

Disappointed: "I thought you would be pleased! This sounds like a wonderful evening to me."

Angry: "What am I supposed to do with these tickets/this video? Why didn't you contact me first?"

Afraid: "What will happen to us? Are we too different? Can we find a way to keep this from happening?"

From compassionate awareness, Theater and Video can both find <u>for themselves</u> great sympathy and understanding.

Each can see and accept their enthusiasm-turned-to-disappointment.

Each can have a gentle, open response to their own wounded feelings, and from that openess, find the same understanding and compassion for the other's feelings.

Sometimes this is followed by a good laugh

If we use awareness
for self-hating purposes,

we will soon cease to look, and
conditioning
self-hate
egocentricity
fear

will trap us in its delusion once again.

BEING RIGHT
(Most of us are pretty attached to it.)

Because of the way we are conditioned as
children, only one person can be right.

If someone close to me disagrees
   with how I see something,
   with what I feel,
   with what I think,
               one of us has to be wrong.

If one of us is wrong,
one of us is not good.
If one of us is not good,
one of us is not lovable.

The belief:
To be right is to be good.
To be good is to be lovable.

A common belief:

If I can just explain my position clearly
enough to you, you will agree with me.

The reason you don't agree is that you
don't understand what I'm saying. You
don't understand because either:
  I haven't been clear, or
  you aren't listening.

It is difficult for us to imagine that
someone can
  understand what we are saying,
  not agree with us,
  have another opinion,

            and still love us.

CONFLICT
(some bad news and some good news)

This is what happens in conflict:

I believe that conflict means my survival is threatened. It isn't logical to an adult mind, but the emotional undercurrent is there and has been since childhood. Its message is:

> "I am in danger!
> I must defend my position."

When both partners feel this way, it is too threatening for either to give up their position and embrace the other's viewpoint.

I am locked in my postures, you are locked  in yours. You are trying to get me to agree that you are right; I'm trying to get you to see that I am right. It is too threatening to each of our identities to let go and move to the other's position. We have no models for:

each of us has a perspective, and
it's okay to see things differently.

Perhaps neither of us is seeing what is so.

We are both acting from conditioning we needed to survive as children; we both feel if either lets the other talk us out of our position, we won't survive.

If we become aware of this, we have the possibility of exploring other perspectives, but not as long as we believe defending our position is necessary for survival.

When, as a 20-, 30-, 40...-year-old,
I am in an intimate relationship
   and I want my life to work
     and I want to be happy,
      it is helpful to know this

I am so ardently defending is, in fact, a
2- or 3- or 4-year-old child's perspective,
and the very thing that enabled me to
survive as a child is now threatening my
survival as an adult.

Now for the **good news** and the **bad news:**

First, the **bad news:**
Built into the survival system is the
resistance to change. Constancy and
permanence are qualities I want in a
system I believe I must have to survive.

This system resists outside influence,

but it also resists
my own attempts
to alter it!

As an adult, I can see that the current
difficulty I'm having with my partner
        is not the real problem--
my internal 3-year-old's survival system
        is the real problem.

But just having that knowledge is rarely
enough to make much of a difference.
Even if I am aware of this, I am unlikely
to let go, although all that is going on is
that you want us to dress up on Saturday
night and go to the theater, and I want us
to stay home and watch a video.

When we are operating out of

fear	a problem
loss	urgency
deprivation	a need to be right

we are identified with the survival system. These are the signals the system sends to make us believe we are being threatened.

If we are both committed to conscious, compassionate awareness (BIG IF), instead of putting a problem between us and fighting over it,

we can place it to the side, move closer together, combine forces, and find a solution that will help us both. There is a place that is most compassionate for all. That's what we're looking for.

As long as we identify with the illusion of being separate,

as long as we believe we are a separate self who is in control,

and as long as we see ourselves as alone,

we will be lonely.

We will try to escape the aching loneliness through many avenues, chief among them, relationship. Even our religion, spiritual practice, faith, and hope can be efforts to escape the emptiness of lonely lives.

But there is no escape.

This is the good news.

So is this... ⇒

As long as I am
maintaining and defending
a separate self,
I will suffer from the loneliness of feeling
separate.

No relationship will give me the closeness,
intimacy, and connectedness
from which identifying
with a separate self
excludes me.

If I am ever to have the relationships I want,
     I must face
squarely this false identity I have spent my life maintaining.
     I must see
through it and face it down.
     I must find
the willingness to stop hiding, defending, pretending, and denying.
     I must see
my conditioning--not myself, for I cannot see myself until I have seen my conditioning--and stop believing it has anything to do with me.

What?

This doesn't sound like **good news** to you? If your interests are freedom and mastery, it does.

☆☆☆

es, I am selfish, arrogant, demanding, impatient, controlling, insensitive, irritable, and self-centered.

Everyone is (depending on who is doing the judging).

We all are until something
SHAKES US UP,

--such as losing a relationship we wanted-- and causes us to find a way to go beyond our egocentric social conditioning and enables us to live in the moment with life exactly as it is.

We might still have all the programmed reactions arise,
but we will no longer believe that they are real
or true
or that we must respond from them.

☆☆☆

The Duality Slide

A concept I ask people to consider is what I call the duality slide or continuum , and here is what I mean by that.

In eastern philosophy it is said that the world we live in is the world of opposites, the world of duality. Generally, this is understood to mean all we perceive is made up of opposing forces:

right/wrong
good/bad
moral/immoral
healthy/sick
beautiful/ugly

When we decide something is right, good, or beautiful, in that moment we create its opposite.

These dualities exist nowhere but in our
minds, are learned in childhood, are crucial
to the maintenance of egocentricity, and
are different for everyone. If we are
unaware of this dualistic, arbitrary mode
of perception, we are doomed to toil
endlessly back and forth between opposites,
between dualities.

should I stay	should I go
am I right	am I wrong
let go	hold on
give in	dig in
say yes	say no

We must see that trying to solve dualistic
problems by trudging back and forth
between opposites leads to endless
suffering and confusion. This will never
result in change.

In Zen, it is said, "When the opposites arise, the Buddha-Mind is lost." We could also say: when we are caught on the duality slide, caught in conditioning, freedom from our suffering is not possible.

Example: Ellen wants emotional connection; Bob wants space. Conflict results. So Ellen decides to be more sensitive to Bob. She's going to give him more

space.

She has seen her "flaws," and is going to improve herself.

She spends some time doing that,
                    and then gets sick of it.

She isn't getting what <u>she</u> wants.

$\Rightarrow$

Here she is so concerned about being the person she should be--

giving, sensitive

--but no one is giving her what she needs in return. She decides to heck with it and moves back to the other side of the duality.

The change Ellen is looking for will not happen in this movement. It can happen only in getting off the continuum, the duality slide.

The change we are seeking will result
from being consciously aware
of the limited nature of our conditioning,
not from switching
from one conditioned reaction to another.

So, with conscious awareness added to the mix, here's another possibility:

Bob and Ellen go away together for the weekend...

Bob is looking forward to some "downtime," some kick-back-and-do-nothin' time. He wants a weekend of quiet relaxation.

Ellen wants to spend the weekend doing things that draw them closer together. She's not too particular about what that might be, she just wants to feel a special connection to Bob.

They reach their destination and conflict begins.

From conscious awareness, both Bob and Ellen can stay in the present, noticing without judgment of any sort that each is looking for something different.

Each can see the fear that arises when it begins to feel like they aren't going to get what they want, and, with that awareness, have compassion for themselves and each other.

A dialogue can start that uncovers expectations neither knew they had.

Anger and disappointment might arise, but from conscious awareness, they can see the old survival system at work.

They can choose to open their hearts and find the place of compassion where both have what they truly want: an intimate, caring relationship.

--If Bob abandons his wishes in order to take care of Ellen, it will not work.
--If Ellen abandons her wishes in order to take care of Bob, it will not work.
--Ignoring, withdrawing, or avoidance will not work.

Compassionate acceptance of self and other and the entire situation
          <u>exactly as it is</u>
will lead Bob and Ellen to freedom.

When difficulties arise in relationship,
how can I:

⇒ move away from reacting out of
unconscious conditioning and move to a
deeper, more conscious, centered, open-
hearted response?

⇒ be less caught up in an emotion,
less convinced that the emotion is true,
real, valid?

⇒ embrace the deeper value of being
present, in the moment, and come from a
place of compassion?

⇒ learn to choose this deeper place,
and, from there, know the conditioned
reactions I learned as a child that are now
threatening my relationship?

⇒ learn not to feel bad about my
conditioned self; not try to justify it; not
try to get rid of it; but from this deeper
place, find the courage to see through the
conditioning and cease to identify with it?

We often confuse a **feeling** with a circumstance. This is an aspect of conditioning that it is critical for us to see through if we are to have happy, healthy relationships.

I rarely hear anyone say, "I am **feeling** anxious." What I usually hear is, "I **am** anxious." Or nervous, insecure, lazy, moody, shy, etc.

Now, at first glance this could seem like a matter of semantics. But when we consider that "I am feeling anxious" conveys acknowledgment of a temporary condition, while "I am anxious" indicates a state of being, the difference is far greater than simple semantics.

"I am feeling anxious"
implies a time when I was not
and the possibility of a time
when I will no longer be.
This is temporary.
This too shall pass.

"I am anxious"
has no such context. This is me,
who I am, my constant state.
I am anxious.
Period.

Here is the real difficulty with not being
aware of a feeling versus a circumstance:

When anxious, I always try to figure out what is making me anxious.

My belief is: "I'm feeling these feelings. Something must be causing them. What is it?"

So I begin to look around. Sometimes I find something right away to pin the feelings on, but if I don't, I continue searching until this belief is satisfied.

If I am doing an awareness practice and paying really close attention, I might see that under certain circumstances I have learned to label

the sensations in my body.

the thoughts in my head,

and my emotional reactions

"anxious."

My stomach is in a knot.

I keep having the same thought over and over.

I feel afraid.

My hands are sweaty.

I feel overwhelmed.

I wish this would just go away.

How can I fix this problem?

I keep clenching my jaw.

With anxiety, the physical sensations,
    resulting thought patterns,
    and emotional reactions
    don't change much.

The **content** of the thoughts
-what I tell myself I'm anxious about-
    changes,
    but the **process** stays the same.

I become obsessed with the content
    and don't notice the process.

I get 100% hooked by "what" I believe I'm
anxious about and never notice
        this is simply what I do!
Until I look into it, it seems obvious that,
"When this happens, I feel this."

The implication is that
    I have no choice.

So, it is helpful to avoid the trap of believing, "I feel anxious because..."

In fact, I feel anxious because I am conditioned to feel anxious and because I have the ability and capacity to feel anxious. My belief is that if I didn't feel anxious under certain conditions, something would be wrong with me.

Feeling anxious at any given time can depend upon conditioning, unconsciousness, lack of attention, stress, hunger, tiredness, nervousness... many things. My proof of this is to notice that
   on THIS occasion,
   under THESE circumstances,
                  I feel anxious.
   On ANOTHER occasion,
   under THE SAME circumstances,
                  I don't.

I don't need to justify my feelings nor do
I need to believe them.
I just need to be aware of them and to
accept and embrace them.

Freedom,

               clarity,

                          and transcendence

lie in comprehending <u>me</u>,
my conditioned beliefs,
how I keep myself separate,
how I cause myself to suffer.

In relationship with self and others it is very helpful to know that:

- when I have these thoughts, and
- when the thoughts trigger these emotions, and
- when I do whatever I do in response to the emotions and thoughts

I am acting out of conditioning, I probably learned this as a child, and I don't have to believe any of it anymore.

Nothing is requiring me to stay stuck in these patterns.

I can let it all go.

It is possible.

Another obstacle to being able to see
through this particular trap of egocentric
conditioning is that we then tend to put
the whole thing on the duality slide:

I'm anxious.
I shouldn't be anxious.
Yes, I should.
No, I shouldn't.

Back and forth,
never noticing that none of this
leads anywhere,
never noticing that the content changes
but the process remains the same.

☆☆☆

Cheri: You begin a relationship with someone who is not exactly the person you want, but they could be.

June: So easily.

Cheri: So very easily.

June: They just need fine-tuning.

Cheri: Yes (laughs). This goes back to childhood. This is what people did to us and what we have learned to do to ourselves and others. They constantly tried to improve us, make us a little better, fix us a little bit here and there.

And now as adults, we have internalized the socialization process. When we are not happy, not getting what we want, we search out what is wrong so we can fix

the problem. Maybe then we will get
what we want, and we'll be happy.

So, here I am in a relationship, and I
decide the other person isn't perfect.
But I am convinced that if I try hard
enough and set a perfect example, I can
make the other person perfect. I can
demonstrate through subtle, discreet,
shrewd, tactful means how to be an open,
warm, vulnerable, loving, honest partner.

This is just swell until I begin to get it
that the other person is not responding.

Perhaps then I redouble my efforts.
Maybe I'm being too subtle and tactful
because if I weren't, surely the person
would understand and be different, right?
Again, this is what we learned from our
parents. And they learned it from theirs,
and so on.

After a while, if I can't "fix" the other person, I'm going to start outright training methods. I will:

withhold affection,
become cold and distant,
snap irritably,
say sarcastic things,
put them down in front of others--

doing to the other person what was done to me to make me be different.

ABANDONING OURSELVES
(We all learned to do it)

 ear of abandonment has
nothing to do with anyone
other than ourselves.
I am convinced of this.

Its origin is in childhood when I learn to
believe that I must make an agreement
to leave myself,
focus attention on someone else,
struggle to be what that person wants,
and try to get from that person what I
need to survive.

My fear of abandonment is not because
my mother wasn't attentive to me, not
because my father didn't give me enough
time, not because of sexual, emotional, or
physical abuse, not because of_____
_____ (Fill in the blank).

⇨

My fear is because of the original abandonment of myself, the "agreement" I made as a child.

Cheri: As children we learn to leave ourselves in order to be and do what someone else wants. This is, in essence, abandoning ourselves and choosing someone else. Sadly, for many this becomes the definition of love.

Will: So if you love someone, you are willing to abandon yourself to do or be what they want?

Cheri: That's right, but it's not even that we are willing. We just do it. No thought involved. And if we don't, at least we feel we should. And it has little or nothing to do with what the other person needs or wants from us. Often it seems all we need or want from one another is the abandonment of self. If you love me, you will abandon yourself for me. If I love you, I will abandon myself for you (and feel all the rage, fear, and shame I felt as a child).

Will: What is being abandoned?

Cheri: My true, authentic, original self. I leave that and look outside myself for what I need and want, for what will make me happy. I leave the authenticity of the moment and respond from conditioning.

And often it's not really "outside." I do this inside. Basically, I move away from that authentic, original self and go to another place inside me, another **identity**.

The problem
NOW
is not what happened
THEN.

The problem
NOW
is I continue to
abandon myself

almost moment-by-moment, for someone
else's opinion, the hope of gaining approval,
a better job, better opportunity, or simply
from habit even when nothing is at stake.

⇨

Example: I seldom interact with the president of the company I work for, but I admire her and want her to like me.

One day I'm sitting in my office, doing what I'm paid to do, kind of enjoying myself, and she shows up unexpectedly. Suddenly I'm self-conscious and ill-at-ease. I am acutely aware of her presence and of my desire to have her approve of my work and like me as a person. I pray that whatever comes out of my mouth is intelligent, amusing, and original. I hope she thinks I'm dressed appropriately, likes my office, hasn't come to give me the ax...

In this, I have left the joy of the moment, of simply enjoying my work, to try to get approval and recognition from someone I hardly know.

If I don't get it, I feel
    rejected,
    disapproved of,
    and abandoned--

        but who abandoned me?!

If I were aware of her presence from **center**, I would probably have a better chance of presenting to her the person I want her to know.

        **It is not true
        that I must abandon myself
        to be an acceptable person.**

We do not
have to abandon ourselves
and try to be a better someone
to connect with another.

The wonderful truth
is that only authentic selves
<u>can connect</u> with each other.

LIVING FROM CENTER

A cornerstone
of the ego
maintenance
system is the

belief that living from center is hard.

People honestly believe it is easier to go
through life ignorant and deluded, even
though they can tell they are suffering.

Living from center is not hard.
It's the easiest thing in the world.

IT'S STRESS FREE.
THERE'S NO AGONIZING,
NO BIG DRAMA,
NO DRAGGING ANYTHING AROUND.
IT'S INCREDIBLY RESTFUL.

It's why people who live from center have
so much energy--there's nothing draining it
away.

And yet,
    egocentricity
    suffering
    fear   } same
    self-hate   thing
    illusion of separation

would have us believe that

        paying attention,
        being aware,

        takes a tremendous toll.

Well, it does take a tremendous toll.
        On egocentricity.

IDENTITY SHIFTS
(You'll probably recognize this one.)

At the beginning of our relationship, I love all the excitement, playfulness, and romance. You do too. We're "singing off the same page," to use a popular expression. I feel as if I am on vacation, and I hope it never ends.

After a while (weeks, months, years?), it begins to feel less like a vacation. In fact, it feels like I have returned home and gone back to work. This exciting, intimate relationship has become a chore much of the time.

In this, I have shifted identities,
    but you have not.
I have come back to being the person I
usually am,
    but you have not.

Perhaps we have both shifted identities,
but our "usual selves"
don't get along as well as our
"in love selves."

Perhaps I have returned to being my
"responsible adult" identity, and you are
now, in my eyes, someone who needs too
much time and attention, and I am not
pleased at having to give you that.

⇨

Wanting you to shift into
another identity
because
I have shifted into
another identity

is a common dynamic in relationship.

Example: Suddenly I decide it's time to:
(choose one) take a month-long vacation,
cut our expenses in half, have children,
buy a helicopter, move to the country.
I have identified with a different part of
myself from the ones you are used to,
and I want to change dramatically the
rules of the relationship as we have
established them. And, basically, I want
you to change into a compatible identity
and go along with me.

If you don't cooperate,

I will almost certainly have the response I learned as a child when this kind of thing happened.

It's Saturday morning and you want to sleep in and then watch cartoons on TV. Dad decides it's time to spruce up the front yard. Mom wants help around the house. You have to get up and accommodate whatever they, the power figures, decide is important to do now.

If you didn't make that shift, what happened? If someone in your family didn't want to change identity, what happened? Fights? Withdrawal? Cold silence?

The chances are very good that the response you learned as a child is the response you have as an adult.

Pete: The example of working in the yard on Saturday morning is exactly the thing that happened when I was a child. There was no choice. I could go without getting a whipping first, or I could complain, get a whipping, and then go. Either way, I went. Now, as an adult, if I want someone to do something I think needs to be done right now, I can get pretty...

Cheri: Heavy-handed?

Pete: Heavy-handed, yes. Thank you.

Cheri: So you have an identity who treats others the way you were treated as a child.

Pete: Yes, many times I find myself acting just like my father, even though I promised myself I never would.

Cheri: This is a clear indication of just how deeply conditioned we are. And, of course, to me the only truly helpful response in these times is compassionate acceptance of all that is going on--all the ways you might be acting that you disapprove of, all the feelings you might be having that disturb you, all the thoughts you might be thinking that sound like your father. Embrace it all, no judgment, and return to center.

PUNISHMENT
(Punishing people does not make them good.)

We SAY we don't want to be manipulative and punishing with an intimate partner, but we <u>do know how</u> to do that. We know how to make their lives so miserable, they WILL do what we want.

And we punish people in much the same way we were punished.

It might not be exact--maybe I was slapped, and I wouldn't slap my partner-- but emotionally, psychologically, spiritually, I know how to punish them.

(If you can't really remember how you were punished as a child, look at how you punish yourself and others now!)

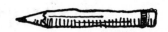

How were you punished as a child?

How did your parents punish themselves?

How did they punish each other?

How do you punish yourself?

How do you punish others?

CONTENT AND PROCESS
(Don't confuse 'em.)

Even though I am beginning to see through the <u>content</u> of my conditioning, I am not able to see the <u>process</u>.

     I don't realize that WHAT I am seeing is not the problem--

> "Oh, I see! I'm too
> self-centered.
> I need to be less selfish."

--it is HOW I am seeing it that is the problem--

> "I'm <u>too</u>* self-centered."
> I <u>need</u>* to be less selfish."

* These are judgments.

I am continuing to use the same
system of conditioning
I learned as a child

to improve myself
as an adult.

It wasn't a good idea then,
and it's not a good idea now.

Once again, the system of conditioning:

In the beginning,
  - I was a particular way,
  - an authority saw that as a wrong/not good way to be,
  - I was punished/rejected/had love and approval withdrawn until I was the way I "should" be.
To avoid the pain of this,
  - I trained myself to be the way I "should" be by watching to see when I was wrong/bad, and
  - I punished/rejected/withdrew love and approval from myself before anyone else had a chance to.

If I bring this approach
to awareness practice,

I am using
the system of conditioning
to try to get out of
the system of conditioning.

It will not work.

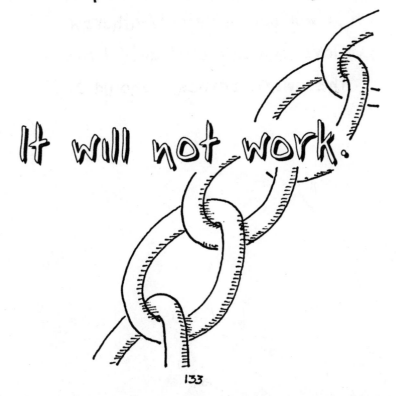

If I come to an awareness practice to
learn
　　what I am doing wrong
　　how I need to change
　　how to be the person I should be
I am simply adopting a new **identity** as
someone who does an awareness practice.

　　Oh, I see! I need to be aware!
　　I will watch myself carefully to
　　see when I am not aware, and
　　　I will punish/reject/withdraw
　　　love and approval until I am
　　　the aware person I should be.

This will be successful only if staying stuck maintaining an identity is what I want to do.

And that is exactly what my egocentric, thoroughly conditioned, separate self wants to do! It says,

"Egocentricity uses self-improvement as self-maintenance. As long as you are concerned about improving yourself, you will always have a self to improve."

There Is Nothing Wrong With You. 1993. Keep It Simple Books, publisher.

So, what is the alternative?

The alternative is

    not trying to fix or change,

    awareness without a goal of self-
      improvement,

    attending minutely, subtly, care-
      fully to the smallest details of
      perception, thought, feeling,
      behavior, and conditioning while
      BELIEVING NOTHING,

    letting go of any idea of <u>control</u>
    or <u>knowing</u> or <u>being right</u>.

This is conscious, compassionate,
passive awareness.

PASSIVE AWARENESS
(Conscious, compassionate awareness: same thing)

When we sit in meditation,
we practice passive awareness.

Not holding on to anything.
Not pushing anything away.
Just sitting.
Just here.
Present. Awake. Aware.
Noticing everything.
Allowing everything to be as it is.
Starting with oneself!

CAUTION

Passive is a word that causes red flags to go up for people. They become quite agitated. That's what people are afraid spiritual practice is, anyway.

They are afraid they will become passive/apathetic/boring/bored.

(In fact, that's what we are when we are following our egos around, although that's not something ego likes us to notice.)

Those who hold these fears are people who have never attempted anything passive. Anyone who has knows how difficult it is.

⇒

Egocentricity is doing.

It is not interested in anything passive.
Forget that, it says. It wants <u>to</u> <u>do</u>
something every moment.

And if there is nothing external <u>to</u> <u>do</u>
something about--

    to fix,
    change,
    or at the very least, judge--

                  there is always oneself.

To clarify what I mean by passive awareness, I use the example of passive solar heating.

The sun shines onto some sort of collector--tiles, barrels of water, stones-- and heats it. The collector stores the heat.

The sun isn't trying to heat the collector, the collector isn't trying to to store the heat, but together they create solar heating. Each is present, and the transformation happens.

In the same way, if I am practicing passive awareness, I am simply here, aware, present.

If I am busy trying
   - to know what's right
   - to know what's wrong
   - to make the best plan
   - to be a good meditator
   - to have great insights
   - to be compassionate
   - (add your own)
it would be very easy to miss the fact
that what is going on

HAS NOTHING TO DO WITH RIGHT OR WRONG OR PLANS OR ANYTHING ELSE. IT DOESN'T EVEN HAVE ANYTHING TO DO WITH ME!

So if I'm practicing passive awareness, I'm
not trying to accomplish anything. I'm
simply aware and present, noticing
everything that happens. Not judging. Not
solving problems. Not making plans.

Example of passive awareness:

Ellen is waiting for Bob to come home and share his day with her. Each day when he comes home, she wants him to talk. He's tired and just wants to relax for a while. She tries to draw him out; he balks; she feels rejected; they fight. Before they've had dinner, the evening is over.

Standard procedure is that she would take classes or begin therapy. She would do all she could to figure out what's wrong with her? with him? with them? Is it something fundamental? Are they just too different? Is the spark gone?

Eventually, Ellen might come to something like this passive awareness we are talking about.

She is not going to assume there is anything wrong with her, him, or the relationship. She is simply going to watch how this happens. She is not going to try to fix anything or solve any problems. She just wants to see how this discord happens.

She begins to watch...

When I'm under stress I sometimes over-react.

When Bob says that, I feel angry.

I judge myself for feeling needy.

I have a belief that he should be more like me.

It's hard to be completely honest with myself and with Bob.

We often misunderstand one another.

What happens then for Ellen? How does "awareness without a goal" help her not suffer in the relationship?

Passive, non-judgmental awareness gives
Ellen a shot at
   leaving her childhood baggage behind,
   slipping into the moment,
   and meeting the challenges of
      intimate relationship
                     from center,
                     wholeness,
                     complete adequacy,
                     and compassion.

From this place, she is not a victim to her
conditioning. She can <u>respond</u> instead of
<u>react</u>. She can <u>be</u> instead of <u>do</u>.

☆☆☆

As long as we are stuck
in the right/wrong
us/them
me/you
good/bad illusion,
we do not have a chance at a larger view.

Social conditioning teaches us to identify
what is wrong and try to improve it to the
point of right.
I am this way.
I need to work on myself
until I am that way.

The problem with this process is that not
all of me wants to improve until I am
"that way." Part of me likes to be this
way, thank you very much. It might not
be pretty, but it's me! Most of us have
at least one stubborn little part with a
how-dare-you-try-to-change-me approach
to all this self-improvement.

Personally, I say thank goodness for that part since it helps us move along more quickly toward the moment of realizing that

skating

back

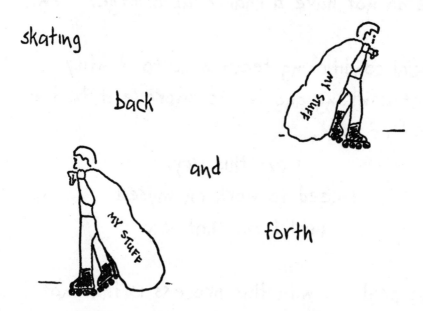

and

forth

on the duality continuum is not going to get us anywhere.

Let's say I realize my relationships don't work because I am <u>controlling</u>.

And so my work is cut out for me.

I must move from the controlling end of the spectrum to the not controlling end, right?

Controlling is bad/wrong.
Not controlling is right/good.

Just like when I was three:

throwing my food was bad/wrong,
not throwing my food was right/good.

And what I learned then, I believe now:

the reason I am not loved
is that I am bad/wrong,

and what I need to do is
improve myself
until I am right/good.

Okay. No problem. I can do this. Had lots of practice.

And so I begin...

Now, I have done a lot of work! I am far less controlling in relationships than I used to be--as long as we don't count the amount of control I am exerting to control myself in situations I used to try to control.

BUT NOW WAIT A MINUTE!!

I don't feel more loved.
In fact, I feel depressed, angry, and resentful.

How can this be?
Maybe I've given up too much here. I'm not so controlling of others, but I certainly feel controlled. Who is making sure I get what I want in life? What about me? Who is going to make sure I am comfortable, have a say, get a vote? I seem to be the only one concerned about not controlling others. Others don't seem too concerned about not controlling me!

So I begin to inch my way back along the controlling/not controlling slide. Perhaps I decide I need a balance. I will have control in some circumstances and relinquish it in others...

So I noodle that for a while, and the old
conditioning sighs a contented sigh and says,
"Ahh, it's good to be home."

I trudge that trail between opposites
over and over.

  have more/have less
  relationship/alone
  live in the country/live in the city
  party animal/stay-at-home

Back and forth. All the way to that side,
snapped back to this side.

  diet/no diet
  on the wagon/off the wagon
  exerciser/couch spud
  meditate/remain ignorant

(I slipped that last one in there to see if
you are paying attention.)

Life seems endlessly varied, and often confusing, because we think each change of content signals a change of process. We believe that when the issue changes, or when we have moved to a different place with the issue, something new is going on.

What if you repeatedly got on a bus marked "want a relationship" and rode to the end of the line, got off, then boarded a bus going the other way marked "want to be alone"? How long might it take you to recognize these two buses? notice that you are in a predictable pattern? begin to find the scenery really familiar? and begin to suspect what is really going on?

"Hey! I think I've been here before!"
Yep. With just about every aspect of life!

Parallel Reality
(a peculiar notion)

A huge part of the maintenance system for egocentric conditioning is the belief in a parallel reality. This original faulty premise from which people can live their whole lives goes like this:

There is an alternate, parallel reality that exists simultaneously with this reality, and in that one, everything is as it should be.

Consider this:
A little child is playing and throws a rock at a tree. The rock ricochets and hits his little brother in the head who begins to scream. Mother is frightened by the screams and rushes out of the house, demanding to know what has happened. Little child senses this is not a good situation. He knows the right explanation

could save him, doesn't know what that is, and goes mute.

Younger brother yells, "He hit me with a rock!" Mother yells, "What is the matter with you? Why did you hit your brother with a rock?"

Little child whimpers, "I didn't mean to. I was aiming at a tree. It bounced off."

Does this work? Is the child off the hook? No way. The response from mother is **the all-time award-winning crazy-maker:**

"You shouldn't have done that.
You should know better."

At first the child is bewildered. He tries to figure out how he could have known something he didn't know. He concludes others must be able to do it, and there must be something wrong with him for not being able to. Finally, he just accepts, "That's right, I should know better."

This is the birth of the parallel reality myth in which:
 I know what I should know
 I do what I should do
 I feel what I should feel
 I look how I should look
 I never forget to remember
 I always make the right decision
 I always say the right thing
 on and on and on...

Here, in this reality, I should know better but don't; there, somehow, I do.

I hope you can see the disastrous effects of this insanity throughout life.

In this way I am able to suffer nearly every moment. If I am constantly comparing this moment with an imaginary moment in which everything is as it should be,

how can I not suffer?

It would serve us well to see that the little child who threw the rock could not have known better, that we never know better, that this is an illusion, an imaginary world perpetuated by looking at a moment that has passed and saying, "It should have been different."

There is no different,
no should,
no better,
no other.

THIS IS IT.

When we are truly present,
really here,
this is all we could ever hope for,
everything it should be.

How Change Happens
(It's probably not what you think.)

As I begin to drop the process of denying my own adequacy, giving it to someone else, and then looking to that person for fulfillment, I decide I am going to be <u>completely different</u> in the next relationship. This is a new day, and I am going to stop following those old, unconscious, conditioned patterns. The time has come.

OLD UNCONSCIOUS CONDITIONED PATTERNS

However, the steps I can take are actually quite small. Those old patterns are my **identity**, and they are devoted to maintaining themselves.

So, no, I am not going to become a different person no matter how much I am able to have an intellectual understanding of "what's wrong with me and how I should be different in order to have what I want."

My survival system is going to protect me from making those kinds of wholesale changes in my identity. I couldn't survive that kind of radical change. I wouldn't know what to do,
how to act,
who to be.

I am protected against those brilliant ideas of just becoming a different person tomorrow.

So I take very small steps...

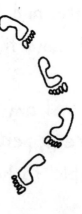

Example: I want a particular present for my birthday, but asking outright for what I want is too uncomfortable for me. My inclination is to drop subtle hints. But the person I'm hinting to isn't getting it.

By hinting in a way that is unclear, I don't get the present, but I do get to feel unloved, unappreciated, ignored, and unhappy.

As I see that this is going on, when it's time for a present, instead of doing my usual steps in the dance, I realize I need to say clearly what I want. The small step I take is to say, "My birthday is next week, and I would like _____."

This will be surprisingly hard. I will feel vulnerable and exposed when I try to break out of the old pattern. Those conditioned responses are going to

rise up really fiercely to try to get me
not to change.

But I remain resolute.

DANGER!

I pick little things I'm going to do, and I
begin to practice two things:

1. Getting clear within myself about what
I want from the other person and asking
for it.

2. Sitting still, literally and figuratively, in
the face of the fear and discomfort that
arises when I do something different from
my conditioning, when I don't do and be who
I'm supposed to do and be.

The _content_ of this example--wanting a certain present--is a small thing in the larger picture,

but the _process_ --remaining **centered** in the face of the fear that accompanies going against my conditioning--

is how the change we are seeking happens.

☆☆☆

ow will passive awareness help me see my conditioned patterns of behavior so that I can make more conscious decisions about how I live my life?

A scenario:
My habit of being late results in discord and unhappiness in my relationships. I am criticized for tardiness, but I dismiss it. People don't know how busy I am. I tried to be on time, but
-the phone rang just as I was leaving.
-someone stopped by the office.
-the kids wouldn't put their shoes on.
-Fred asked me to iron his shirt.
-I lost my watch.
-I'm time challenged.

I argue, defend, yell and get yelled at, lose friendships, lose jobs, feel stressed--and then one day it all comes together and

I GET IT!

I DON'T WANT TO BE LATE!

My partner just looked at me with hurt and defeat, and, in a second, emotionally moved a million miles away from me.

The day is ruined, and I really get it.
I DO NOT WANT
TO DO THIS ANYMORE.

Now, my usual approach is to resolve that this will never happen again, but I know that doesn't work. I've tried resolutions, and the result is that before long I'm miserable and tense, and soon after, I fail. So I'm going to try some of this awareness stuff.

I know I won't have long to wait for my first chance to practice since I'm late all the time!

(And I'm not going to beat myself up, because I've read <u>There Is Nothing Wrong With You</u>, and I know beatings don't help. Besides, as the book says, if beating myself up for being late worked, I'd be punctual by now.)

I'm just going to watch.
Notice.

So I start, and I begin to see how my conditioning undermines my resolve to achieve my goal.

For example, I need to meet my boss at his office across town in half an hour.

A voice in my head says, "But you're so close to finishing this memo. If you take two more minutes, you will be done with it and it can go out. You know he wanted this done today."

Ten minutes later I look at my watch. "Oh no, I'm going to be late!"

The voice says, "It's okay. You can make it. It's only twenty minutes in traffic, and traffic is light this time of day."

As I'm racing for the door, papers flying from my briefcase, the phone rings. I look back. "No, I don't have time to answer it. But what if it's the boss? I'd better answer it. Hello. Oh, Mom, I can't talk now, I'm late. Yes, Mom, I know I'm always late, but I'm working on it. No, I've really got to go. I'll call you tonight. 'Bye. Fifteen minutes. I can't believe it."

Suddenly, I'm overwhelmed by exhaustion. "I'll never make it if I don't have a cup of coffee. I know I don't have time, but..."

After watching a few of these episodes,

I begin to see
how conditioning
sets me up
to maintain itself.

I see that it talks me into being late, and because I believe <u>it</u> is <u>me</u>, I wind up defending it! It makes me late, and then I defend my actions to my boss, or I fight with my loved ones, telling them how they should be all right with what my conditioning does to me and to them.

The first step in turning this around is ceasing to feel bad. I just "came to," just got here, just became conscious, and I don't know what's going on yet. Blaming myself for what happened when I was unconscious is just another way to stay unconscious. My commitment is to waking up so these things don't happen so often. Once again, I don't need to try to change--trying to change keeps the system in place--I need to wake up, and I will be different, I will already have changed.

The second step is listening to and sorting out the voices. Which ones lead me toward waking up, toward consciousness, and which ones lead me to remain in conditioning, in unconsciousness? I can find out which is which by watching the results I get when I do what it says.

The voice talks me into doing one more thing, brings in anxiety about what might go wrong, how I might get into trouble, fear of retribution, plans to take care of me that don't really take care of me (answer that call, get that coffee), and I begin to see how that voice sets me up for the experience it claims to be saving me from! Got it!

The third step is to practice not believing the various
voices, not getting
pulled in or thrown
off by them.
I need to focus,
stay present,
breathe,
be right here in this moment,
pay attention.
One breath at a time.

I need to be somewhere in half an hour,
I need to leave right now. But what
about... No! I need to leave right now!
        Breathe in, breathe out.

It is important to notice that at no time
in this awareness process is it necessary
to involve anyone else.
Not the boss,
        not your friends,
            not your partner.
                No one.

To use a partner as an example, of
course when you are late he sighs his long
suffering sigh. You want to tell him how
hard you've been working on punctuality.
You want to say how much better you are
now than you used to be, how unfair and
insensitive he is for not noticing.
                    Don't do it.

When you are no longer late, he will notice.

It is important to keep in mind that you are doing this for you.
The benefit to the relationship is secondary.

Again, the content of this example-- being late--is relatively insignificant, but recognizing the process--how our conditioning sets us up to fail-- is a giant step toward freedom.

☆☆☆

I hear from people that the awareness I
suggest seems hard to them, it requires
so much

time   and   energy.

If we consider how much time and energy
we spend repeating the same old
unsuccessful patterns,

simply paying attention
with a fresh mind and
a lack of assumptions
to find out what is really going on
          might not seem so hard.

Being Still

You draw the
← illustration.

Being still burns
away conditioning.

Avoiding, denying, explaining, rationalizing,
comparing, trying to escape, hoping for a
better future, feeling guilty about the
past--all these are learned responses that
create and perpetuate suffering.

Just being still, staying through it, being
present, creates a fire, an energy that
literally burns away our desire to continue
our old patterns.

Example: I say something thoughtless and
your feelings are hurt. Now conditioning
jumps in to fix it. "Oh no, I'm sorry. You
misunderstood. I didn't mean it the way it
sounded."

If you accept my apology (accept like a good, conditioned child that your perception is wrong), I can go back to sleep until the next time I'm jolted awake by the pain my actions have triggered in someone.

But if I don't let an apology take care of it, if I don't try to convince you that what just happened

>   didn't happen,

if I sit still with your hurt feelings, my distress, the pain and suffering of unconsciousness and conditioning,

>   I just might
>   be less willing and
>   less likely to go to
>   sleep and let it
>   happen again.

Becoming still is vastly different from being still. ⇒

Becoming still is a future event that will never happen. ⇒

Being still is a present state that can include becoming still. ☆

Example: I'm trying to be calm. I am working at being a calmer person. Meanwhile my identity is as a person who is not calm. But I'm working on it...
My identity is safe because that future time in which I am calm will never arrive.

However, if I can expand the circle of acceptance to include my lack of calm, I can be calm about the whole issue and achieve NOW the calm I was hoping to reach in the future.

"But I can't be calm about not being calm."

Then the issue isn't calm, it's control.
"I will be calm as soon as everything is the way I want it to be."

Now that's a whole different discussion!

Be aware,
without judgment,
of how you are.

Be aware,
without judgment,
of the world you have created.

Without rationalization
or recrimination,

be quietly aware.

Cheri: When my teacher told me I was to leave the monastery and conduct workshops, I was in a rough spot because I felt unprepared and ill-suited for the job.

Fortunately (although it didn't feel fortunate at the time), there were only two possible responses to his requests: yes or goodbye. Since I didn't want to end my monastic training, I risked telling him how fearful I was of teaching from a Zen perspective, not to mention speaking in front of groups of people.

His guidance to me when I expressed my misery was,

> "You will do for the love of others
> what you would never be willing
> to do for yourself."

Those words have guided me over the years, and it occurs to me that they express the potential that exists for us in relationships. Sometimes it is most apparent with a child. Even when we are unhappy with something the child has done, we can easily see the
purity and innocence,
and we are moved
to greater love and openness. (We **project** our own purity and innocence onto the child.)

In intimate relationship, at the beginning we can usually see our partner's purity and innocence because we are open and undefended with each other. (**Projection**, again. Those qualities in ourselves are being reflected in the partner.) Then, just as in childhood, when we start receiving the blows, the disappointments, the hurts, we start to close off...

But, as adults, if we can go beyond our conditioning, stay open-hearted, and not put up defenses,

If I don't stick to my position, she'll think she can control me.

I'm not going to listen to you until you change your tone of voice

I don't need him. I'll do it by myself.

I'm convinced he does this just to make me mad. I'll ignore him.

She's irrational. I'm going to go drink beer with my buddies until she calms down.

if we can continue to see the other person from that original, innocent, pure place,

we have the opportunity to heal much injury and suffering.

AND IN GOING BEYOND OUR
CONDITIONING FOR SOMEONE ELSE,
WE LEARN TO GO BEYOND IT
FOR OURSELVES.

Don't struggle to change.

Struggle strengthens
what you are trying to change.

One part of you thinks another part of
you should be improved, and you fall into
the trap of believing you need to change.
But who is making the judgment?

Conflict between these opposing desires
wears down the willingness to be present.

Ego tries to change ego.
Ego struggles against ego.
Ego resists ego.
Ego fights back.
Ego wins!

"You" lose in every conflict.

When we try to escape
where we are,

we create the duality,
the comparison,
that causes our suffering.

What if you were just fine
the way you are?
Ego, fear, self-hate,
would lose its grip on you,

wouldn't it?

Linda: Instead of being happy and then looking for someone to share that with, I look for somebody to make me happy. This doesn't work well at all.

Cheri: It reminds me of the example we put in one of our other books about the woman who was devoted to marrying a rich man. Well, okay, she could do that, but

she is ignoring such things as compatibility, respect, shared values and ideas. She is clearly looking for something external she believes she needs to be happy.

From our perspective, this woman would be far more likely to get what she wanted if she found her own "treasure house" and projected from there.

It's the first principle of **projection**: what you see is who you are. If you are wealthy within, you see wealth all around you. If you feel lacking and deprived, all the money in the world won't make you feel wealthy.

If I am looking for
a relationship to make
me happy, **to give me**
what I won't give myself,
I am almost certainly headed for
disappointment.

Why?

If I am unable to do these things for myself, no other person will ever be able to give me enough to ensure I have a lasting sense of well-being. That just does not come from the outside. Only I can truly do that for myself.

opular culture, movies, magazines, TV, music, novels, etc., often portray a single person as inadequate and unfulfilled in some way. The remedy for this woeful state, they tell us, is intimate relationship. Only through relationship with another is a person likely to get what they want out of life.

WHAT AN INCREDIBLE BURDEN!

It is a burden on the other person to expect them to

help me through all the hard things,
take me out of my bad moods,
pick me up when I am down,
make me feel better,
give me what I don't have.

It is scary for the other person to think
they have to meet all these needs
for me.

It is scary for me to think I would need
someone to take care of me
in all those ways.

It is even scarier to think

someone wants that stuff from ME!

We look to relationship to give us what we are missing in the rest of our lives.

My responsibility in relationship is to be a whole person.

I can take care of myself,
  meet my own needs,
  make myself feel better,
  be who I want to find.

From this place of wholeness and well-being, I can share life with another person who is also devoted to being whole.

It's a sharing,
  not a taking.

It's a receiving,
  not a grasping.

A woman asked me recently, "When you do a practice like this, do you reach a point where you don't want a relationship?"

As always, my response was it's not that you won't <u>want</u> a relationship. It's very likely you will want all kinds of relationships. The difference is you won't <u>need</u> them. You won't think you are lacking anything a relationship would give you.

This is what we mean when we say, "One process does not lead to another."

"Wanting" does not lead to "having."
Wanting leads to wanting.
Having leads to having.

<u>Wanting</u> a relationship that will cause you <u>to have</u> a certain feeling will not work.

If you want to feel a certain way,
feel it

now.

Looking forward to a time

when that will happen

will result only

in looking forward to a time

when that will happen.

he relationship that is idealized by egocentricity is based on dreams and myths and false ideas. It is based on delusion and suffering. Even though it is fun to begin with, it has about as much substance as a Las Vegas show or a ball of cotton candy. Drinking a lot of alcohol can be fun; waking up the next day isn't. Eating a lot of rich, spicy food for dinner can be fun right up until you get in bed and try to go to sleep. Quick, sexual involvement with someone can follow this same pattern-- "the morning after" syndrome.

It is very hard for us to see the depth of the con job conditioning is laying on us.

⇒

In relationship it gets particularly tricky, and here's why:

I am not going to feel
anything in a relationship
I don't feel outside one.

> And everything I feel
> outside a relationship,
> I will feel while in one.

Without a relationship, I feel lacking, incomplete, inadequate, unfulfilled, and dissatisfied. I believe that when I am with someone, things will be different, I will be happy, complete, satisfied, etc.

> No, I won't.

The relationships I've been in prove that over and over again. I tend to forget this truth because, in the beginning, I am distracted. I am pulled out of my habitual

identity and thrown into another identity--
the one who loves to buy flowers, have
romantic dinners, wear different clothes,
go to special places.

This is a particular identity. It is not "who
I normally am." It is not the person I was
before this "temporary derangement," and
it won't be who I am when I pass through
this derangement.

Example: I'm just going along day to day,
a person with a certain orientation to life,
a certain "affect," as the world of
psychotherapy might say. And then
I buy a new red
convertible on
the first day of
summer, and my "affect" goes out the
window! Suddenly I'm a risk-taker, a bon
vivant, a free spirit.

But how long does this last?
Pretty soon either the summer is over,
or the car gets dented, or I have just kind
of lost my ability to be excited by this
particular possession, and I go back to
being who I was before.

Now, many of us just go on to the next
thing. "Okay. All right. I need... a house
on the beach... a different job... a new
relationship... Yeah, that's it! There's no
spark in this one (read: it's no longer
mirroring me the way I want to see
myself). In fact, not only is it not bringing
out all the wonderful feelings it once did
(back when I was the way I really am--
exciting, adventuresome, and thrilling), it's
making me grouchy and irritable and more
and more dissatisfied. Clearly I need to
find a new person, someone who makes
me feel like the person I really am."

With this system, I am operating in a world
of delusion. There is
no car,
    no job,
        no house,
            no person
who is going to alter that fundamental
orientation I have to life. That orientation
will be altered only by an internal process.
We call that process awareness practice or
self-discovery.

I begin to drop habitual patterns of
suffering and delusion, and I spend more
time here in the present, in a place of
clarity, seeing how I maintain suffering, and
letting it go.

                From that place,
                  I am different.

The how-to of the movement
from looking outward
to looking inward
is called
"moving into conscious awareness"
or
"paying attention."

And remember:
When we begin to look at ourselves in this
new way, the first question conditioning asks
is, "What do I do? I can see my
relationships in the past have not been
successful, and I can see I am at the root
of the problem because I am the
constant. I have related to all kinds of
people, and I come to the same places
inside myself over and over. My suffering
comes from inside me, and I want to
address that. WHAT DO I DO?"

This question is a trick.

In effect, it is asking, "How do I get rid of these things in myself? How do I become the person I should be?"

Once again, this is what happened in childhood. We learned to look at ourselves so that we could
    see what was wrong with us
    fix the problems
    be who we should be,
    be lovable,
    get what we wanted.

Now, as adults, we do this analyze-and-fix, judge-and-correct process in almost every aspect and moment of our lives.

This is like going

to your closet and

trying to change

who you are by

throwing out all

your old outfits

and replacing them with new ones.

We are suggesting that switching habits,
beliefs, feelings, and behaviors is like
changing clothes...

It won't take you
                    where you want to go.

            What we are looking for
              is inside the heart.

We find it by
     being still,
     bringing our attention to the moment,
     seeing how we cause our suffering,
     and letting it go.

                ☆☆☆

 Cheri: If I can't have the relationship with myself that I want someone else to have with me, I need to give up on the idea of relationship. As well as I know myself--my concern for others, my willingness and sincerity, my determination to be a good person--if I don't think I am lovable, why do I think someone else will? If I don't see that having a loving relationship with myself is worth any effort it might take to achieve, I need to accept that I'm never going to have it and get on with whatever I'm going to do as an alternative.

Here is the secret to the whole thing, I think: if I see myself as worthy and lovable, and if I act in the world from that place, people will see and respond accordingly.

This might lead to having the relationship I want, and it might not.
             Either way,
        I will have the life I want.

It is important to remember that when I am lonely, I am separate from ME, not from someone else.

When I prove to myself that I am a person who is worthy of love, who is loving and lovable and worthy of being in the kind of relationship I want to have, that's the place I'm going to operate from in the world. Other people are going to recognize it, too.

Jean: When I think of having that relationship with myself, and when I think of others seeing that within me, my motivation becomes the fact that they will be attracted to me! So ego takes my noblest intention and twists it into something completely self-serving.

Cheri: Egocentric conditioning (conditioned mind, "I", self-hate, fear, illusion of separation) takes everything and twists it. Count on it.

That's why we don't waste time and energy trying to fix or get rid of conditioning. That's why the only work we ever do is moving back to **center**. Whenever we find that we have been out in conditioning and suffering, coming back into this moment, getting present, that's all we ever do.

We are never going to change conditioning.
We are never going to
  satisfy dissatisfaction,
  make inadequacy feel adequate,
  make fear unafraid,
  make deprivation feel fulfilled.

It's never going to happen, folks!

If we GET THAT, we can stop focusing on it, stop feeling bad about it. Of course egocentricity is going to twist everything you do and think and decide. Of course it's going to take any life-affirming, compassionate, freedom-producing plans you make and turn them into reasons to stay stuck. That's just what it does.

So, is there anything wrong with you for having this conditioning? No. Everyone has it. Is there anything wrong with any of this? No, there isn't. All we need to do is take a breath and come back to center, to this moment.

I recognize this is seldom as easy as I present it to be.
Simple, yes; easy, no.
It takes practice.

If you were drowning, and I said all you have to do is roll over on your back and float, well that's pretty simple. But if you don't know how to do that, you're still drowning. So, what you want to do very quickly is learn
<u>to roll over on your</u>
<u>back and float</u>!

Okay,
so there you are.
You decide you want a romance in your
life. Maybe you already have one, but it's
no longer fulfilling. Instead of trading the
person in, or spending your life lamenting
the fact that you don't have a relationship,
you catch on that

THE PRIMARY RELATIONSHIP
IN LIFE IS THE ONE
YOU HAVE WITH YOURSELF!

It is the first and most intimate.

So you become for yourself
the person you want to find.

How do you create this relationship with yourself?

You get into the moment and you don't compare it with anything else. You don't go into the conditional, imaginary world of,
"This would be so wonderful
if I could share it with someone."
Instead, you are simply in the moment with yourself, enjoying exactly what is happening there.

The relationship we are pointing at comes from the conscious awareness of center.

It might not have
the same fireworks,
but it is much deeper
and broader and more satisfying.
And before long you'll realize it does have fireworks, they just look different from center.

EXERCISE:

Describe the steps you would take,
the gifts you would buy,
the generosity you would bestow,
the kindness you would offer,
the enthusiasm you would have,
the attention you would give,
and anything else that appeals to you,
if you were to begin giving to yourself the
things you want someone else to give you.

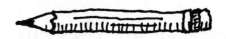

This is nirvana,
this is samsara.
This is heaven,
this is hell.

When we are conscious, it's one experience; when we are unconscious, it's another.

Relationship is heaven,
relationship is hell.

When we are conscious, it's one experience; when we are unconscious, it's another.

As I tell people, it's a case of mistaken identity.

We need to move
from the stage
to the audience.

The practice of **passive awareness**, awareness without a goal, shows me my blind spots, the places where I thoroughly believe the stuff that goes through my head, the unexamined nonsense that runs great portions of my life.

I am in a relationship and my partner or spouse:

is usually late
is inordinately tidy
is tight with money
isn't affectionate enough
is too lenient with the children
sulks instead of talking
_____ (add your own)

We struggle until I finally get to the place where I am just going to be aware and see if I can know what is going on. This is ruining our relationship and a part of me knows it's silly that a relationship could be ruined over something like this. So I watch, I pay very close attention.

These are the kinds of things a person might see:

I notice that I feel chaotic when this is going on. I feel out of control, disrespected. "You know how much this means to me. If you loved me you would _____. But you don't, and so it is obvious that you have no respect for me, you don't care about my feelings, and you don't love me."

As I watch, I begin to realize that these things are not true. It's all **conditioning**.

Feeling chaotic is conditioning.

Believing that tidiness/punctuality/ discipline/ talking/_____ is superior is conditioning.

Concluding that you don't love me because we have different standards is conditioning.

Feeling disrespected because you won't do what I want you to do is conditioning.

And, ultimately, having an attachment to one side of ANY issue is conditioning.

And at the deepest level I realize that my conditioning is my responsibility. It's what causes me to suffer. It's not actually anyone else's beliefs or behaviors. It's not how the world works or how life is. It's my conditioning that makes me suffer, that causes me to close my heart, that gives me problems in relationships. At the deepest level I know it is my responsibility to deal with this.

How do I "deal with this," you might ask?

I see that the **sensations** in my body,
the **thoughts** in my head,
and my **emotional responses** to the sensations and thoughts

are all conditioned--I learned ALL of it.

I walk in and the house is a mess...

I watch the **sensations** arise
and realize they don't mean what I have
thought they mean.

(Ah, tightness in jaw; ah, heaviness in chest)

I hear my **thoughts**
and realize they aren't "true."

(Ah, looking for someone to blame)

I feel the **emotions** arise
and know I don't have to act on them.

(Ah, sadness; ah, anger)

Many of you are thinking, "This is all very nice, Cheri, **but what do I do?"**

The exciting news is that

when you no longer believe your conditioned responses, you are free to do or not to do anything.

Suddenly, you have options. The whole world of possibilities is open to you.

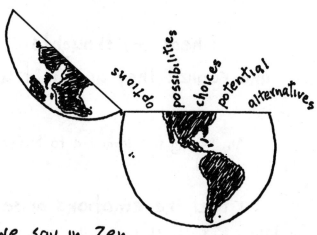

And as we say in Zen,
keep paying attention.

The Zen Center offers workshops and retreats based on the material in Cheri Huber's books. Topics includes depression, projection, aspects of the self, attention and awareness, meditation practice, and many others.

Cheri conducts retreats of varying lengths and formats throughout the U.S. and beyond.

For a current Zen Center schedule or other information, please contact:
Zen Center
PO Box 91
Mountain View, CA 94042
(415) 966-1057

To subscribe to the quarterly newsletter, In Our Practice, send $12.00 cash or check and your name and address to the above address.